FLAG BLOCK
29 x 18″   1776

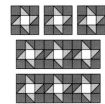

Make 36

Make 9

Make 1

Cutting

For 9 star units:

Background	36 squares 1½″	
	*18 squares 1⅞″	
Star points	*18 squares 1⅞″	
Centers	9 squares 1½″	

*Cut in **half** diagonally.

For stripes:

Light	3 pieces 2 x 14½″	
	2 pieces 2 x 23½″	
Dark	3 pieces 2 x 14½″	
	2 pieces 2 x 23½″	

For frame:

Sides	2 pieces 2 x 18½″
Top & bottom	2 pieces 2 x 23½″

For side unit:

Plain strip	1 piece 1½ x 18½″
Triangle units	
Light	*5 squares 2⅞″
Dark	*5 squares 2⅞″

*Cut in **half** diagonally.

Directions

Use ¼″ seam allowance unless otherwise noted.

1. Make 1 flag block as shown. Press.

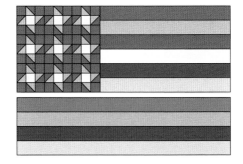

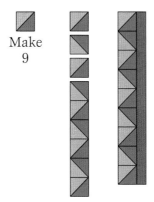

Make 9

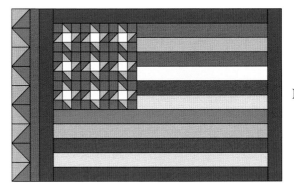

Make 1

4

UNCLE SAM BLOCK
12 x 36″   1776

Cutting

Measurements are given **width by height** as pieces appear in finished block. Background pieces appear in separate sections, and they are in order from top to bottom of Uncle Sam block.

For hat/head section:

Background	2 pieces 3⅝ x 4″ - by hat top
	2 pieces 3½ x 1½″ - by hatband
	2 pieces 2⅛ x 1½″ - by brim
	2 pieces 3¼ x 3¾″ - by face
Hat	1 piece 4¼ x 4″ - top
	1 piece 7¼ x 1½″ - brim
Hatband	1 piece 4½ x 1½″
Face	1 piece 5 x 3¾″
Eyes, mustache, beard	page 39

For upper body section:

Background	2 squares 1½″ - shoulders
	2 pieces 1 x 7⅞″ - by sleeves
Sleeves	2 pieces 2¼ x 7⅞″
Vest	2 pieces 3¼ x 7⅞″
Lapels, stars	page 39

For lower body section:

Background	2 squares 1½″ - hands
	2 pieces 1¼ x 3″ - by hands
	2 pieces 2¾ x 13½″ - below hands
	2 pieces 2 x 1½″ - by pants cuffs
Hands	2 pieces 2 x 3″
Prairie points - vest	2 squares 3¼″
Shirt cuffs	2 pieces 2¾ x 1⅞″
Pants cuffs	2 pieces 4 x 1½″
Pants	
Fabric 1	6 pieces 1 x 17⅜″
Fabric 2	4 pieces 1⅛ x 17⅜″

For shoes section:

Background	2 squares 1½″ - toe
	2 squares 1⅛″ - heel
	2 pieces 1⅜ x 2½″ - sides
	1 piece ¾ x 2½″ - center
Shoes	2 pieces 3¼ x 2½″ - main
	2 pieces 1¾ x 2½″ - heel

Side background strips:

Background	2 pieces 1½ x 36½″

Directions

Use ¼″ seam allowance unless otherwise noted.

1. Make 1 Uncle Sam block as shown. Press.

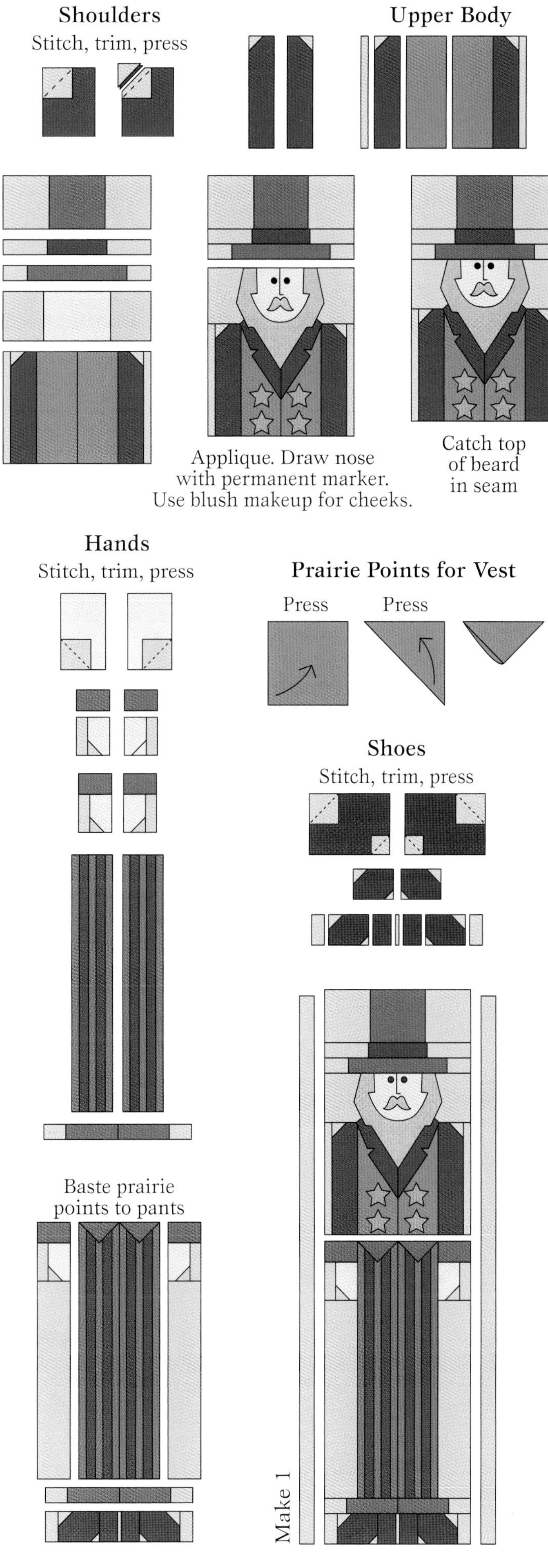

Shoulders
Stitch, trim, press

Upper Body

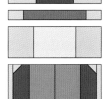

Applique. Draw nose with permanent marker. Use blush makeup for cheeks.

Catch top of beard in seam

Hands
Stitch, trim, press

Baste prairie points to pants

Prairie Points for Vest

Press   Press

Shoes
Stitch, trim, press
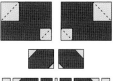
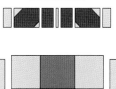

Make 1
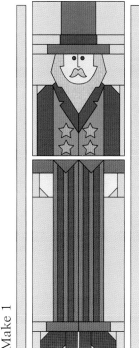
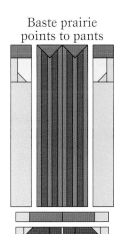

5

IMPORTANT: The layout of this quilt requires that each element be pieced accurately for all parts to fit. **At the beginning of the directions for each element, the FINISHED SIZE of that element, not including seam allowance, is given. WIDTH of block or unit appears first, then height.** We use fusible web applique, so our patterns are reversed and ready to be traced. Be sure to have plenty of fusible web on hand.

55 x 76″

Yardage

Choose fabrics with 42″ usable width.

Orange	¼ yd each of 8 or more fabrics, mediums & darks
	½ yd - witch background
Blue-purple	⅜ yd each of 4 or more fabrics, mediums & darks
	⅓ yd - pumpkin background
	¼ yd very dark - bat
Red-purple	¼ yd each of 5 or more fabrics, mediums & darks - incl Happy Haunting bkg
	⅓ yd - candy corn background
Black	¼ yd each of 3 or more fabrics
	½ yd - wreath background
	⅜ yd - sashing
	⅜ yd - shoes, dress, hat, lapels
Lime green	⅙ yd each of 2 or more fabrics
Turquoise	⅙ yd each of 3 or more fabrics
	⅓ yd - bat background
Yellow	⅛ yd - hair
White	⅛ yd - bat fangs, candy corn
Red	⅛ yd - bat eyes
Dark gray	⅛ yd - bat feet
Brown	⅛ yd each of 2 - pumpkin stem
Black, purple	¼ yd each - checkerboard units
Black	¼ yd - Border 1
Red-purple	½ yd - Border 2
Orange	½ yd each of 2 fabrics - Border 3
Black	⅝ yd - Border 4
Binding	⅔ yd
Backing	3¾ yd
Batting	61 x 82″

Directions

Read through all directions before beginning. Choose fabrics using photo on page 7, then cut large and long pieces such as applique backgrounds and frames before cutting remaining pieces.

Use ¼″ seam allowance unless otherwise noted.

1. PATCHWORK BLOCKS & UNITS: Cut and stitch patchwork blocks and units on pages 14-21 and 8-9.

   ☐ 3 Nine-patch star blocks

   ☐ 4 Four-patch star blocks - 4″
   ☐ 2 Pinwheel blocks
   ☐ 1 Log Cabin block
   ☐ 1 Bars unit
   ☐ 1 Four-patch star block - 8″
   ☐ 4 Checkerboard sashing units
   ☐ 2 Patchwork heart blocks
   ☐ 1 Broken Dishes block
   ☐ 2 Bear Paw blocks
   ☐ 2 Border 3 units
   ☐ 1 House block - bottom row
   ☐ 2 Flying Geese units
   ☐ 1 Houses block - center of quilt
   ☐ 1 witch block

2. APPLIQUE BLOCKS: Use photo on page 7 as a guide for placement.

   ☐ Candy corn block
   Patterns on pages 39, 45
   Cut background 9½ x 8½″
   Applique BOO (pattern on page 45) later - see assembly directions, Step 3, page 22

   ☐ Bat block
   Patterns on page 45
   Cut background 19½ x 8½″

   ☐ Pumpkin block
   Patterns on page 46
   Cut background 10½″ square

   ☐ Wreath block
   Patterns on page 39
   Cut background 12½″ square
   From 5 x 7″ piece of fused fabric, cut 4 **bias** pieces ¼ x 6½″ for vine - use dotted lines for placement

   ☐ Happy Haunting block
   Patterns on page 47
   Cut background 10½ x 6½″
   Applique after quilt center is completed, Step 3, pages 22-23

3. ASSEMBLY & BORDERS: See pages 22-23.

4. LAYER & QUILT: Piece backing horizontally to same size as batting. Layer and quilt as desired. Trim backing and batting even with quilt top.

5. BIND: Cut 8 strips (selvage to selvage) 2½″ wide. Stitch strips end to end. Press in half lengthwise, wrong sides together. Bind quilt using ⅜″ seam allowance.

HOUSES BLOCK
29x18″ Boo!

Make
28

Make
7

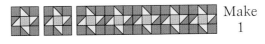

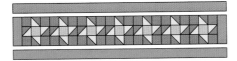
Make
1

Cutting

For 7 star units (3″):

Background	28 squares 1½″
	*14 squares 1⅞″
Star points	*14 squares 1⅞″
Centers	7 squares 1½″

*Cut in **half** diagonally.

For star unit frame:

Sides	2 pieces 1½ x 3½″
Top & bottom	2 pieces 1½ x 23½″

For 4 houses (5½ x 9½″):

Background	8 pieces 1 x 5½″
	beside house
	4 pieces 2 x 6″
	above house
Roof	paper-piecing pattern page 41
Siding	8 pieces 2 x 5½″
	4 pieces 2 x 1¾″
Window	4 pieces 2 x 1¾″
Door	4 pieces 2 x 3″
Chimney	applique pattern page 47

Paper-piecing
pattern on pg 41

Applique chimney.
Pattern on page 47.

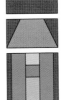

Make 4

For houses unit inner frame:

Sides	2 pieces 1 x 10″
Bottom	1 piece 1 x 23½″

For houses unit outer frame:

Sides	2 pieces 2 x 18½″
Top & bottom	2 pieces 2 x 23½″

For side unit:

Plain strip	1 piece 1½ x 18½″
Triangle units	
Light	*5 squares 2⅞″
Dark	*5 squares 2⅞″

*Cut in **half** diagonally.

Make
9

Directions

Use ¼″ seam allowance unless otherwise noted.

1. Make 1 houses block as shown. Press.

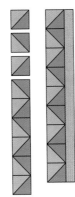

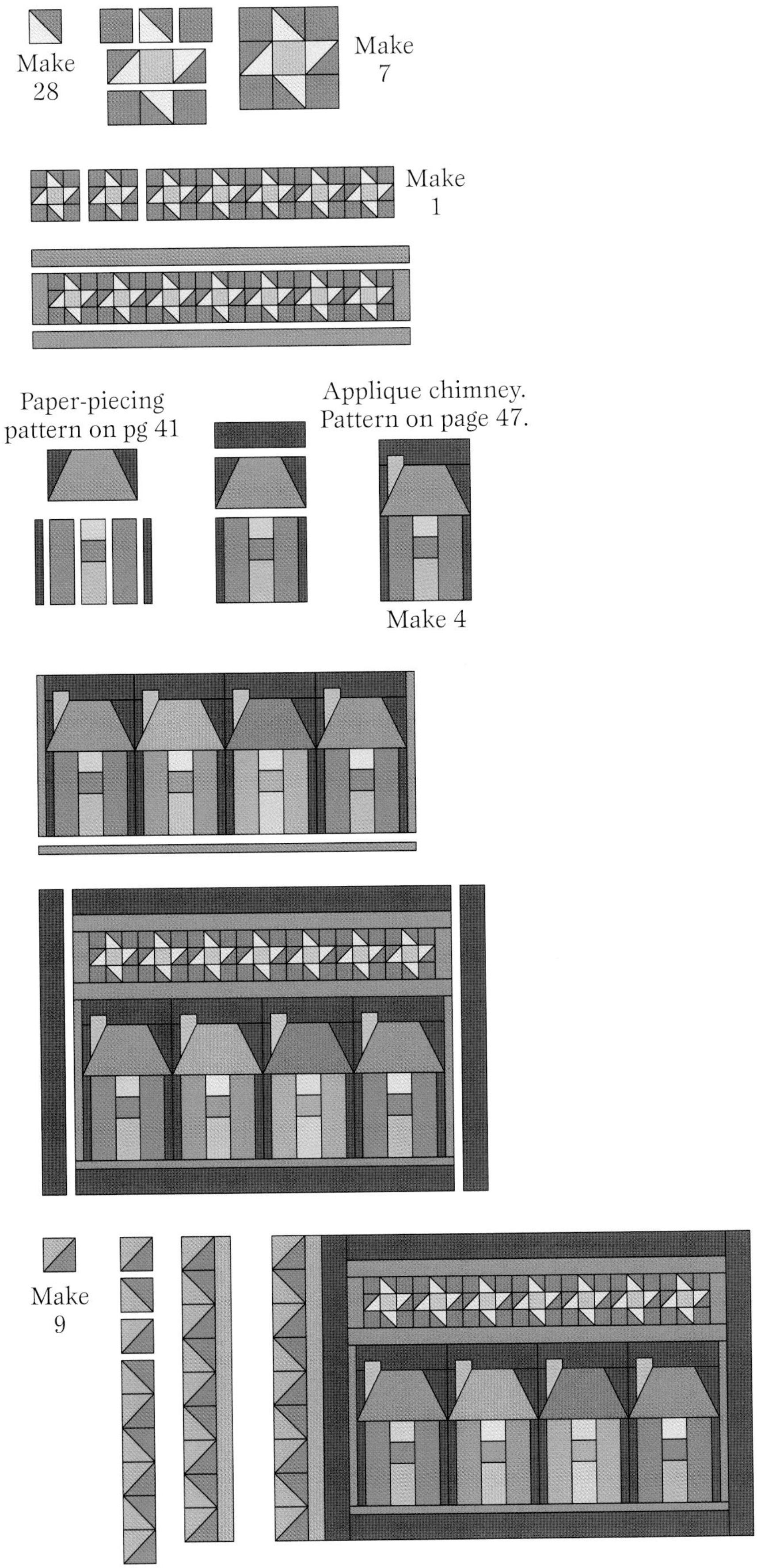

8

WITCH BLOCK
12x36″ Boo!

Cutting

Measurements are given **width by height** as pieces appear in finished block. Background pieces appear in separate sections, and they are in order from top to bottom of Witch block.

For hat/head section:

Background	2 pieces 2⅛ x 1½″ - by hat brim
	2 pieces 3¼ x 3¾″ - by face
Hat	paper piecing - page 44
	stars - page 45
Hat brim	1 piece 7¼ x 1½″
Face	1 piece 5 x 3¾″
Hair	page 47

For upper body section:

Background	2 squares 1½″ - shoulders
	2 pieces 1 x 7⅞″ - by sleeves
	2 squares 1½″ - hands
	2 pieces 1¼ x 3″ - by hands
Sleeves	2 pieces 2¼ x 7⅞″
Vest	2 pieces 3¼ x 7⅞″
Prairie points - vest	2 squares 3¼″
Dress midsection	1 piece 6 x 4⅜″
Dress cuffs	2 pieces 2¾ x 1⅞″
Hands	2 pieces 2 x 3″
Stars, eyes, lapels, buttons	pages 46, 47

For lower body section:

Background	2 pieces 3 x 12″ - below hands
	2 squares 2¾″ - by legs
	4 pieces 1 x 2¾″ - by sides of socks
Skirt	1 piece 10½ x 11¼″
Socks Fabric 1	2 pieces 1 x 2¾″
Fabric 2	4 pieces 1⅛ x 2¾″

For shoes section:

Background	2 squares 1½″ - toe
	2 squares 1⅛″ - heel
	2 pieces 2⅜ x 1½″ - by upper
	2 pieces 1⅜ x 2½″ - by lower
	1 piece ¾ x 3½″ - center
Shoes	2 pieces 3½ x 1½″ - upper
	2 pieces 3¼ x 2½″ - lower
	2 pieces 1¾ x 2½″ - heel

Side background strips:

Background	2 pieces 1½ x 36½″
Spider	page 47

Directions

Use ¼″ seam allowance unless otherwise noted.

1. Make 1 witch block as shown. Press.

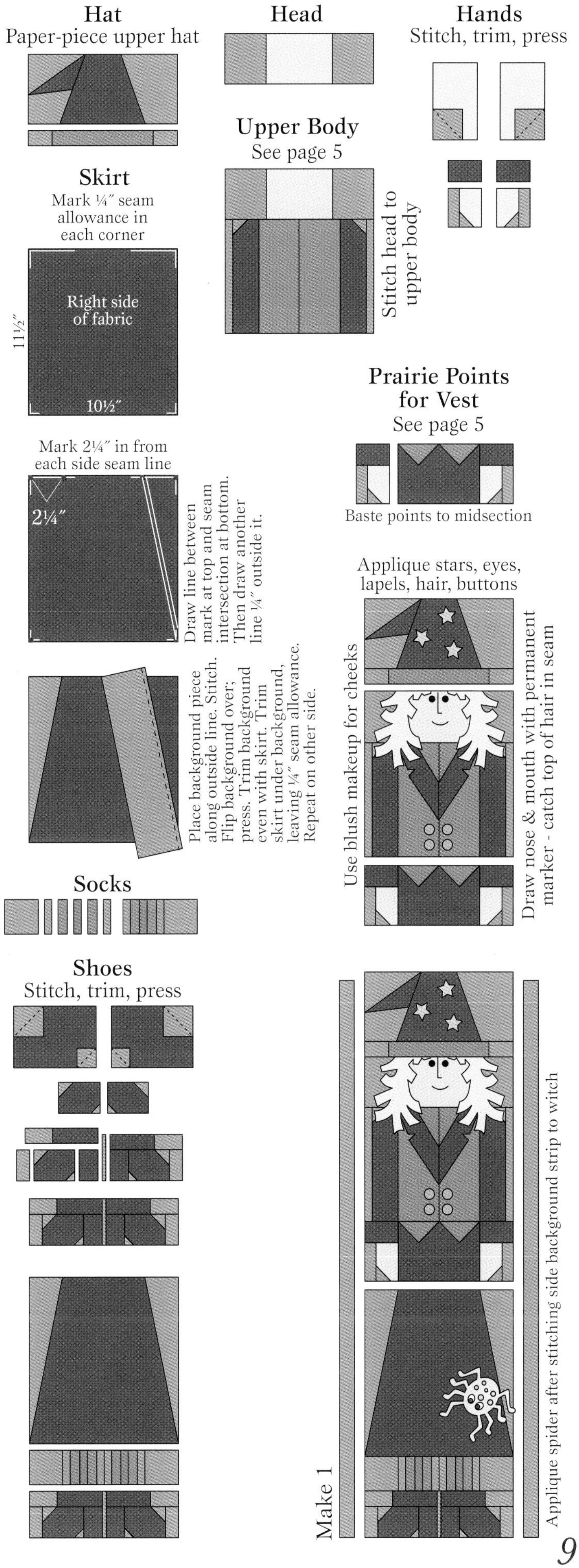

Hat
Paper-piece upper hat

Head

Hands
Stitch, trim, press

Upper Body
See page 5

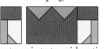

Stitch head to upper body

Skirt
Mark ¼″ seam allowance in each corner

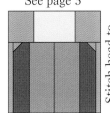

11½″

Right side of fabric

10½″

Mark 2¼″ in from each side seam line

2¼″

Draw line between mark at top and seam intersection at bottom. Then draw another line ¼″ outside it.

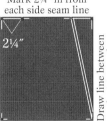

Place background piece along outside line. Stitch. Flip background over; press. Trim background even with skirt. Trim skirt under background, leaving ¼″ seam allowance. Repeat on other side.

Prairie Points for Vest
See page 5

Baste points to midsection

Applique stars, eyes, lapels, hair, buttons

Use blush makeup for cheeks

Draw nose & mouth with permanent marker - catch top of hair in seam

Socks

Shoes
Stitch, trim, press

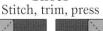

Make 1

Applique spider after stitching side background strip to witch

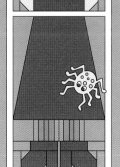

9

IMPORTANT: The layout of this quilt requires that each element be pieced accurately for all parts to fit. **At the beginning of the directions for each element, the FINISHED SIZE of that element, not including seam allowance, is given. WIDTH of block or unit appears first, then height.** We use fusible web applique, so our patterns are reversed and ready to be traced. Be sure to have plenty of fusible web on hand.

55 x 76″

Yardage

Choose fabrics with 42″ usable width.

Red	¼ yd each of 16 or more fabrics, mediums & darks
	⅜ yd - Santa Suit
	⅓ yd - bell background
Green	⅙ yd each of 12 or more fabrics, mediums & darks
	⅓ yd - heart flower background
	½ yd - sashing, lettering
	½ yd - wreath background
Tan/gold	¼ yd each of 6 or more fabrics includes Peace on Earth background
	½ yd - Santa background
	⅓ yd - angel background
Yellow	⅛ yd - wings, halo
Black	⅙ yd - shoes, belt, roof, eyes
Brown	⅛ yd each of 3 fabrics - trees block, hair
Cream	⅛ yd - cuffs, hat trim
Flesh	⅙ yd - faces, hands, feet
Gray	¼ yd - beard, mustache
	⅛ yd - buckle
Black, red	¼ yd each - checkerboard units
Gold	½ yd - Border 2
Black	⅞ yd - Borders 1 & 4
Binding	⅔ yd
Backing	3¾ yd
Batting	61 x 82″

Directions

Read through all directions before beginning. Choose fabrics using photo on page 11, then cut large and long pieces such as applique backgrounds and frames before cutting remaining pieces.

Use ¼″ seam allowance unless otherwise noted.

1. PATCHWORK BLOCKS & UNITS: Cut and stitch patchwork blocks and units on pages 14-21 and 12-13.

- ☐ 3 Nine-patch star blocks
- ☐ 4 Four-patch star blocks - 4″
- ☐ 2 Pinwheel blocks
- ☐ 1 Log Cabin block
- ☐ 1 Bars unit
- ☐ 1 Four-patch star block - 8″
- ☐ 4 Checkerboard sashing units
- ☐ 2 Patchwork heart blocks
- ☐ 1 Broken Dishes block
- ☐ 2 Bear Paw blocks
- ☐ 2 Border 3 units - use assorted red scraps
- ☐ 1 House block
- ☐ 2 Flying Geese units
- ☐ 1 Trees block
- ☐ 1 Santa block

2. APPLIQUE BLOCKS: Use photo on page 11 as a guide for placement.

- ☐ Heart flower block
  Patterns on page 39
  Cut background 9½ x 8½″

- ☐ Angel block
  Patterns on page 42, 43
  Cut background 19½ x 8½″

- ☐ Bell block
  Patterns on page 40
  Cut background 10½″ square

- ☐ Wreath block
  Patterns on page 39
  Cut background 12½″ square
  From 5 x 7″ piece of fused fabric, cut 4 **bias** pieces ¼ x 6½″ for vine - use dotted lines for placement

- ☐ Peace on Earth block
  Patterns on pages 37, 41
  Cut background 10½ x 6½″
  Applique after wreath section is completed, Step 2, page 22

3. ASSEMBLY & BORDERS: See pages 22-23.

4. LAYER & QUILT: Piece backing horizontally to same size as batting. Layer and quilt as desired. Trim backing and batting even with quilt top.

5. BIND: Cut 8 strips (selvage to selvage) 2½″ wide. Stitch strips end to end. Press in half lengthwise, wrong sides together. Bind quilt using ⅜″ seam allowance.

PEACE ON
EARTH
GOODWILL
TO MEN

TREES BLOCK
29x18″ Joy

Cutting

For 7 star units (3″):

Background	28 squares 1½″
	*14 squares 1⅞″
Star points	*14 squares 1⅞″
Centers	7 squares 1½″

*Cut in **half** diagonally.

For 3 trees (7x9″):

Background	3 pieces, 3 pieces reversed - page 41
	6 pieces 3½x2¼″
Tree	3 pieces, 3 pieces reversed - page 41
Trunk	3 pieces 1½x2¼″

For frames:

"Earth"	1 piece 1½x21½″
Inner frame	
Top & bottom	2 pieces 1½x21½″
Sides	2 pieces 1½x15½″
Outer frame	
Top & bottom	2 pieces 2x23½″
Sides	2 pieces 2x18½″

For side unit:

Plain strip	1 piece 1½x18½″
Triangle units	
Light	*5 squares 2⅞″
Dark	*5 squares 2⅞″

*Cut in **half** diagonally.

Directions

Use ¼″ seam allowance unless otherwise noted.

1. Make 1 trees block as shown. Press.

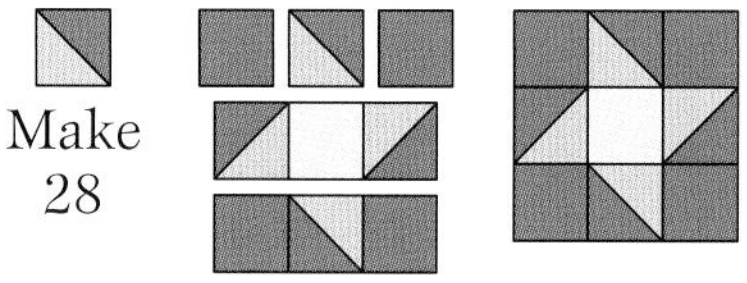

Make 28

Make 7

Make 1

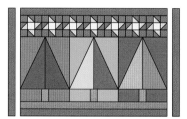
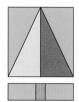

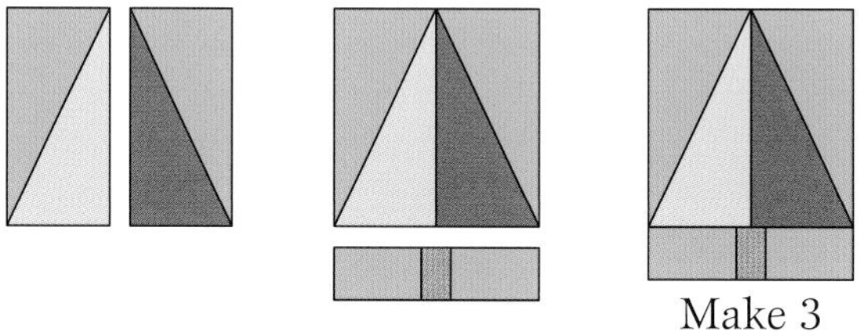

Make 3

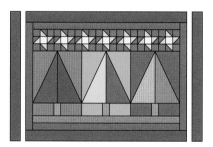

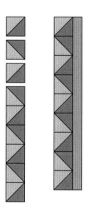

Make 9

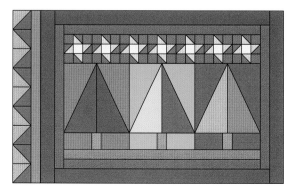

Make 1

SANTA BLOCK
12x36″ Joy

Cutting

Measurements are given **width by height** as pieces appear in finished block. Background pieces appear in separate sections, and they are in order from top to bottom of Santa block.

For hat/head section:

Background	2 pieces 2⅛ x 1½″ - by hat cuff
	2 pieces 3¼ x 3¾″ - by face
Hat & background	paper piecing - page 44
Hat cuff	1 piece 7¼ x 1½″
Face	1 piece 5 x 3¾″
Eyes, mustache, beard	page 39

For arm sections:

Background	2 squares 1½″ - shoulders
	2 pieces 1 x 7⅞″ - by sleeves
	2 pieces 1¼ x 3″ - by hands
	2 squares 1½″ - hands
	2 pieces 2¾ x 13½″ - below hands
Hands	2 pieces 2 x 3″
Sleeves	2 pieces 2¼ x 7⅞″
Jacket cuffs	2 pieces 2¾ x 1⅞″

For body/leg section:

Jacket	2 pieces 3¼ x 7¼″ - upper
	2 pieces 3¼ x 6″ - lower
Jacket flaps	page 37 - cut 4
Belt	1 piece 6 x 3¼″
Buckle, buttons	page 42
Pants	
Fabric 1	6 pieces 1 x 9¾″
Fabric 2	4 pieces 1⅛ x 9¾″

For cuffs section:

Background	2 pieces 2 x 1½″
Pants cuffs	2 pieces 4 x 1½″

For shoes section:

Background	2 squares 1½″ - toe
	2 squares 1⅛″ - heel
	2 pieces 1⅜ x 2½″ - sides
	1 piece ¾ x 2½″ - center
Shoes	2 pieces 3¼ x 2½″ - main
	2 pieces 1¾ x 2½″ - heel

Side background strips:

Background	2 pieces 1½ x 36½″
Hat trim	page 42

Directions

Use ¼″ seam allowance unless otherwise noted.

1. Make 1 Santa block as shown. Press.

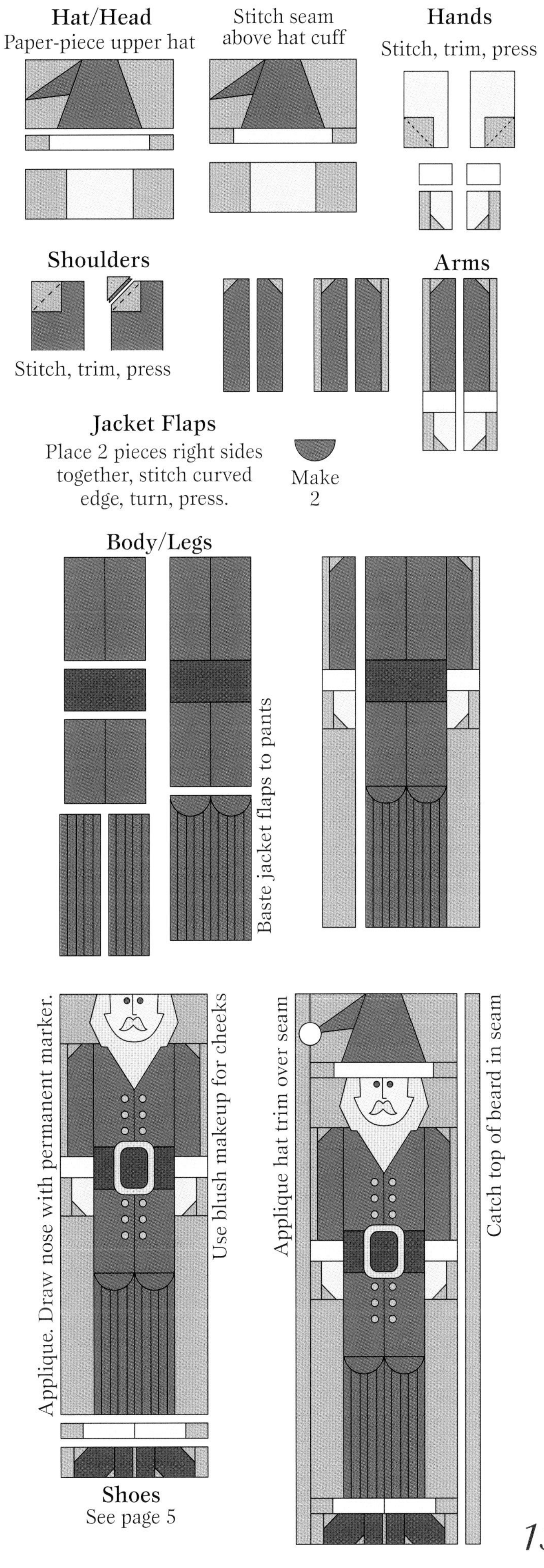

Hat/Head
Paper-piece upper hat

 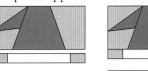

Stitch seam above hat cuff

Hands
Stitch, trim, press

Shoulders

Stitch, trim, press

Arms

Jacket Flaps
Place 2 pieces right sides together, stitch curved edge, turn, press.

Make 2

Body/Legs

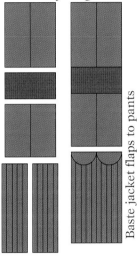

Baste jacket flaps to pants

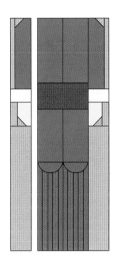

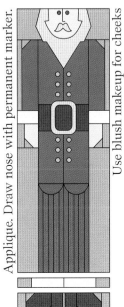

Applique. Draw nose with permanent marker.

Use blush makeup for cheeks

Applique hat trim over seam

Catch top of beard in seam

Shoes
See page 5

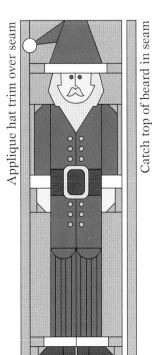

13

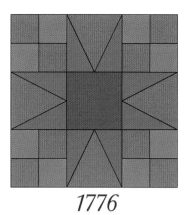

1776

Boo!

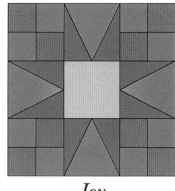

Joy

Cutting

For 3 blocks:

Center	3 squares 3½"
Star points	24 squares 3½"
Star point unit background	12 squares 3½"
Four-patch unit	
Fabric 1	24 squares 2"
Fabric 2	24 squares 2"

Directions

Use ¼" seam allowance unless otherwise noted.

1. Make 3 blocks as shown. Press.

For each block:

Star point squares - mark on wrong side

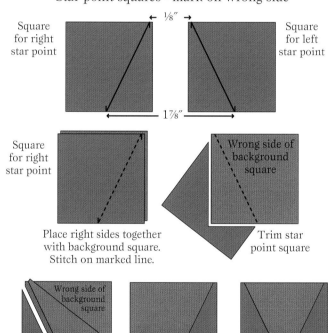

Square for right star point

Square for left star point

Square for right star point

Wrong side of background square

Place right sides together with background square. Stitch on marked line.

Trim star point square

Fold back top & bottom layers. Trim center layer leaving ¼" seam allowance.

Right star point

Repeat for left star point. Make 4

Make 4

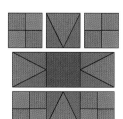

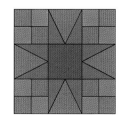

FOUR-PATCH STAR BLOCK 4"

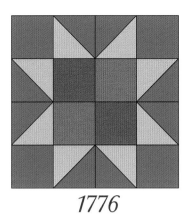
1776

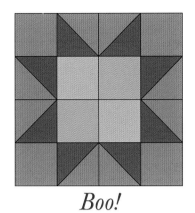
Boo!

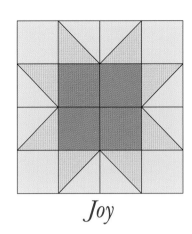
Joy

Cutting

For 4 blocks:

Center fabric 1	8 squares 1½"
Center fabric 2	8 squares 1½"
Star points	*16 squares 1⅞"
Background	16 squares 1½"
	*16 squares 1⅞"

*Cut in **half** diagonally.

Directions

Use ¼" seam allowance unless otherwise noted.

1. Make 4 blocks as shown. Press.

For each block:

Make 8   Make 4

Make 1

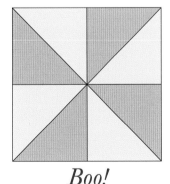 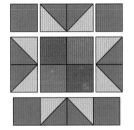

PINWHEEL BLOCK 4"

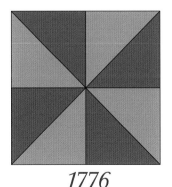
1776

Boo!

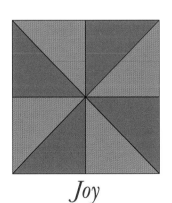
Joy

Cutting

For 2 blocks:

Fabric 1	*4 squares 2⅞"
Fabric 2	*4 squares 2⅞"

*Cut in **half** diagonally.

Directions

Use ¼" seam allowance unless otherwise noted.

1. Make 2 blocks as shown. Press.

For each block:

Make 4

15

LOG CABIN BLOCK 8"

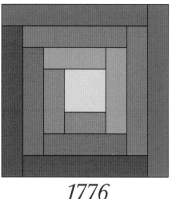

1776

Boo!

Joy

Cutting

For 1 block:

Center, fabric 1	1 square 2½″
Round 1, fabric 2	1 piece 1½ x 2½″
	1 piece 1½ x 3½″
Round 1, fabric 3	1 piece 1½ x 3½″
	1 piece 1½ x 4½″
Round 2, fabric 4	1 piece 1½ x 4½″
	1 piece 1½ x 5½″
Round 2, fabric 5	1 piece 1½ x 5½″
	1 piece 1½ x 6½″
Round 3, fabric 6	1 piece 1½ x 6½″
	1 piece 1½ x 7½″
Round 3, fabric 7	1 piece 1½ x 7½″
	1 piece 1½ x 8½″

Directions

Use ¼″ seam allowance unless otherwise noted.

1. Make 1 block as shown. Press.

For each block:

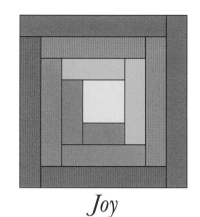

Round 1

Fabric 1   Fabric 3

Fabric 2

Round 2

Fabric 5

Fabric 4

Round 3

Fabric 7

Fabric 6

BARS UNIT 10x4"

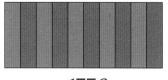

1776

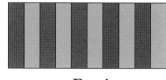

Boo!

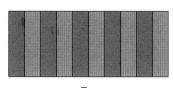

Joy

Cutting

For 1 unit:

Fabric 1	5 pieces 1½ x 4½″
Fabric 2	5 pieces 1½ x 4½″

Directions

Use ¼″ seam allowance unless otherwise noted.

1. Make 1 unit as shown. Press.

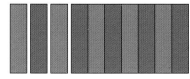

Make 1

FOUR-PATCH STAR BLOCK 8″

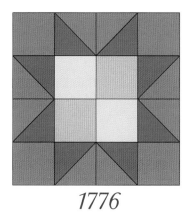

1776

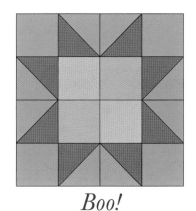

Boo!

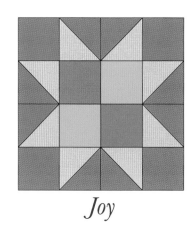

Joy

Cutting

For 1 block:

Center fabric 1	2 squares 2½″
Center fabric 2	2 squares 2½″
Star points	*4 squares 2⅞″
Background	4 squares 2½″
	*4 squares 2⅞″

*Cut in **half** diagonally.

Directions

Use ¼″ seam allowance unless otherwise noted.

1. Make 1 block as shown. Press.

For each block:

 Make 8   Make 4

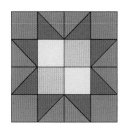

Make 1

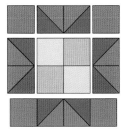

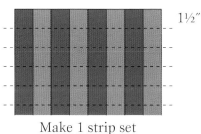

CHECKERBOARD UNIT 41x1″

Cutting

For 4 units:

Fabric 1	*4 strips 1½″ wide
Fabric 2	*4 strips 1½″ wide

*Cut selvage to selvage

Directions

Use ¼″ seam allowance unless otherwise noted.

1. Make 1 strip set as shown. Press.

2. Cut into 1½″ segments.

3. Sew 5 segments together, alternating colors where they join. Unsew a square from a remaining segment and stitch it to one end of unit to make it 41 squares long. Make 4.

1½″

Make 1 strip set

Make 4 units

PATCHWORK HEART BLOCK 6″

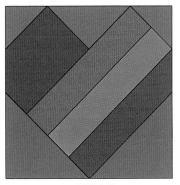

1776

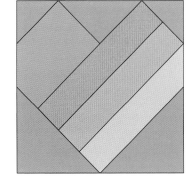

Boo!

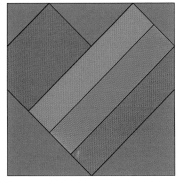

Joy

Cutting

For 2 blocks:

Background #1	1 square 2¾″
	*2 squares 4⅝″
Background #2	1 square 2¾″
	*2 squares 4⅝″
Heart fabric #1	2 pieces 2¾ x 3½″
Heart fabric #2	2 pieces 1½ x 5¾″
Heart fabric #3	2 pieces 1½ x 5¾″
Heart fabric #4	2 pieces 1½ x 5¾″

*Cut in **half** diagonally.

Directions

Use ¼″ seam allowance unless otherwise noted.

1. Make 1 block with background fabric #1 and 1 block with background fabric #2. Press.

For each block:

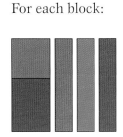

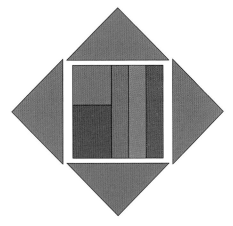

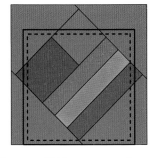

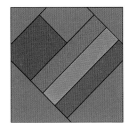

Center 6½″ square ruler or template from side to side & line up bottom edge on raw edge of block. Trim.

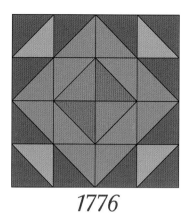

1776

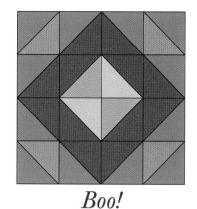

Boo!

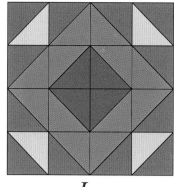

Joy

Cutting

For 1 block:

Background	*6 squares 3⅜″
Center fabric #1	*1 square 3⅜″
Center fabric #2	*1 square 3⅜″
Remaining block fabric #1 - corner unit	*2 squares 3⅜″
Remaining block fabric #2 - center & side units	*6 squares 3⅜″

*Cut in **half** diagonally.

Directions

Use ¼″ seam allowance unless otherwise noted.

1. Make 1 block as shown. Press.

For each block:

 Make 4 for corners

 Make 2 for center

 Make 8 for sides

 Make 2 for center

Make 4
2 with center fabric #1
2 with center fabric #2

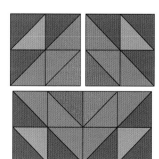 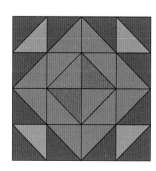

BEAR PAW BLOCK 10½″

1776

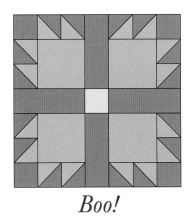

Boo!

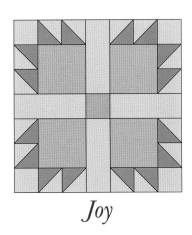

Joy

Cutting

For 2 blocks:

Background	8 pieces 2 x 5″
	8 squares 2″
	*16 squares 2⅜″
Paws	8 squares 3½″
Claws	*16 squares 2⅜″
Center	2 squares 2″

*Cut in **half** diagonally.

Directions

Use ¼″ seam allowance unless otherwise noted.

1. Make 2 blocks as shown. Press.

For each block:

Make 16

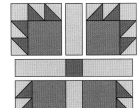

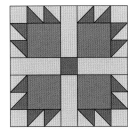

Make 4

BORDER 3 2 x 72″

Cutting

For 2 borders:

Fabric 1 OR dark scraps	36 pieces 2½ x 4½″
Fabric 2 OR medium scraps	72 squares 2½″

Directions

Use ¼″ seam allowance unless otherwise noted.

1. Make 2 borders of 18 units each as shown. Press.

For each unit:

Stitch   Trim   Repeat

Make 2

HOUSE BLOCK 10x10½"

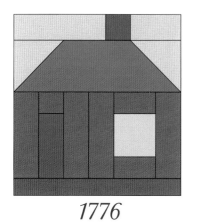

1776

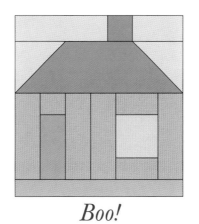

Boo!

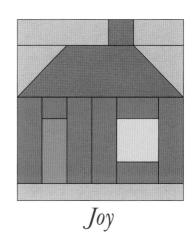

Joy

Cutting

For 1 block:

Background	2 squares 3½"
	1 piece 2 x 6"
	1 piece 2 x 3½"
Chimney	1 piece 2 x 2"
Roof	1 piece 3½ x 10½"
Siding	4 pieces 2 x 5½"
	1 piece 2 x 1¾"
	2 pieces 3 x 1¾"
Door	1 piece 2 x 4¼"
Window	1 piece 3 x 3"
Bottom piece	1 piece 1½ x 10½"

For each block:

Stitch Trim Repeat

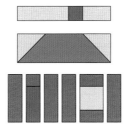

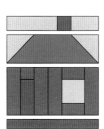

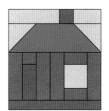

Directions

Use ¼" seam allowance unless otherwise noted.

1. Make 1 block as shown. Press.

FLYING GEESE UNIT 5x10½"

Cutting

For 1 unit & 1 unit reversed:

Large triangles - geese	4 pieces 3 x 5½"
Small triangles - sky	8 squares 3"
Pieces above & below triangles	4 pieces 1¾ x 5½"
Top pieces	2 pieces 2½ x 5½"
Bottom pieces	2 pieces 1½ x 5½"

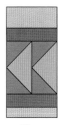

1776 **Boo!** **Joy**

Directions

Use ¼" seam allowance unless otherwise noted.

1. Make 1 unit and 1 unit reversed, as shown. Press.

Stitch Trim

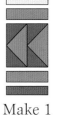

Repeat Make 4 Make 1 Make 1

ASSEMBLY & BORDERS
1776 • Boo! • Joy

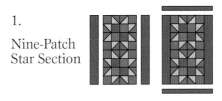

1.
Nine-Patch
Star Section

Cutting Cut strips selvage to selvage.

SASHING

Nine-patch star section	4 pieces 1½ x 8½"
	4 pieces 1 x 6½"
	2 pieces 1½ x 9½"
	2 pieces 1¾ x 41½"
Wreath section	1 piece 1½ x 12½"
Uncle Sam section	2 pieces 1½ x 10½"

BORDERS

Border 1	4 strips 1½" wide
Border 2	4 strips 2½" wide
Border 3	made on page 20
Border 4	7 strips 2½" wide

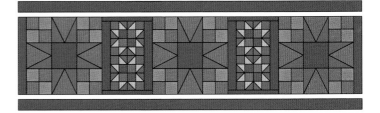

Directions

Use ¼" seam allowance unless otherwise noted.

1. NINE-PATCH STAR SECTION: Stitch star section together using sashing pieces in order listed. Press.

2. PINWHEELS, WREATH, UNCLE SAM (WITCH, SANTA), AND BEAR PAW SECTIONS: Stitch blocks and sashing together in order shown. Applique Let Freedom Ring (Peace on Earth) blocks. (Wait until end of Step 3 to applique Happy Haunting on Boo!) Press.

3. ASSEMBLE: Using diagram on page 23, and adding checkerboard units and flag (houses, trees) block, assemble quilt center. Applique USA (BOO) below heart flower (candy corn) block after seam between pinwheels section and flag (houses, trees) block is sewn. (Applique Happy Haunting on Boo! after quilt center is complete.) Press.

4. BORDERS 1-3: Make sure Border 3 units are the same length as quilt center. Adjust if necessary. Stitch Border 1 strips end to end and trim to same length as Border 3 units. Make 2. Repeat with Border 2 strips. Stitch Borders 1, 2 and 3 together for each side of quilt. Press. Stitch to sides of quilt, oriented as shown. Press.

5. BORDER 4: Stitch Border 4 strips end to end and trim to same width as quilt. Stitch to top and bottom of quilt. Repeat at sides of quilt. Press.

2. Pinwheels Section

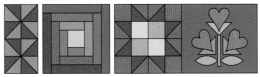

2. Wreath Section

2. Bear Paw Section

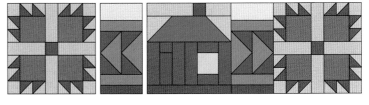

22

2. Uncle Sam Section

3.

4.

NORTHERN LIGHTS

56 x 77″   10½″ Block

Yardage *Choose fabrics with 42″ usable width.*

Background	2 yd - dark
Paws, centers	⅙ yd each of 12 fabrics - medium-darks
Claws	⅛ yd each of 12-18 fabrics - mediums & brights, including some zingers
Border 1	⅜ yd - bright
Border 2	1½ yd - can be same dark as background
Binding	⅔ yd
Backing	4⅞ yd
Batting	62 x 83″

Cutting *Cut strips from selvage to selvage.*

Background	96 squares 2″
	96 pieces 2 x 5″
	*192 squares 2⅜″
Paws	96 squares 3½″
Centers	24 squares 2″
Claws	*16 squares 2⅜″ from each of 12 fabrics - or total of 192 squares
Border 1	6 strips 1½″ wide
Border 2	7 strips 6½″ wide
Binding	8 strips 2½″ wide

*Cut in **half** diagonally.

Directions

Use ¼″ seam allowance unless otherwise noted.

1. BLOCKS: Make 24 blocks as shown. Press.

2. ASSEMBLE: Stitch blocks into rows as shown. Press. Stitch rows together. Press.

3. BORDER 1: Stitch strips end to end and trim to same length as quilt. Make 2. Stitch to sides of quilt. Press. Repeat at top and bottom of quilt. Press.

4. BORDER 2: Repeat Step 3.

5. LAYER & QUILT: Piece backing vertically to same size as batting. Layer and quilt as desired. Trim backing and batting even with quilt top.

6. BIND: Stitch binding strips end to end. Press in half lengthwise, wrong sides together. Bind quilt using ⅜″ seam allowance.

1. For each block:

Make 16

Make 8

Make 4

Make 8

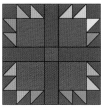

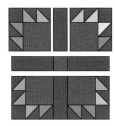
Make 24

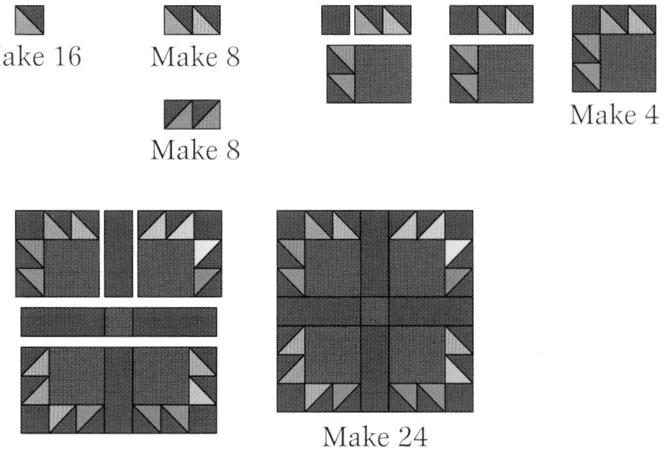

2.

25

20 x 48″

Santa

Yardage Choose fabrics with 42″ usable width.

Background	½ yd
Jacket, hat, pants	⅜ yd
Dark pants stripes, checkerboard	⅛ yd
Beard, mustache, buckle	¼ yd
Cuffs, hat trim	⅛ yd
Face, hands	⅙ yd
Shoes, belt, eyes, checkerboard	⅙ yd
Buttons	⅛ yd OR 12 buttons - ½″
Star unit background	⅙ yd
Star unit points & centers	⅛ yd each of 2 fabrics
Border 1	⅙ yd
Border 2	¼ yd
Border 3	⅓ yd each of 2 contrasting fabrics
Binding	⅜ yd
Backing	1⅝ yd
Batting	24 x 54″

Cutting Cut strips from selvage to selvage.

Santa block	see Step 1
Star units	32 squares 1½″ - background
	*16 squares 1⅞″ - background
	*16 squares 1⅞″ - star points
	8 squares 1½″ - centers
Checkerboard units	24 squares 1½″ - each fabric
Border 1	3 strips 1½″ wide
Border 2	4 strips 1½″ wide
Border 3	24 pieces 2½ x 4½″ - dark fabric
	48 squares 2½″ - light fabric
Binding	4 strips 2¼″ wide

*Cut in **half** diagonally.

Directions

Use ¼″ seam allowance unless otherwise noted.

1. BLOCKS & UNITS: Make Santa block using directions on page 13. Make eight 3″ star units using diagrams on page 4. Make 4 checkerboard units with 12 squares each.

2. ASSEMBLE: Stitch center panel together as shown on page 27. Press.

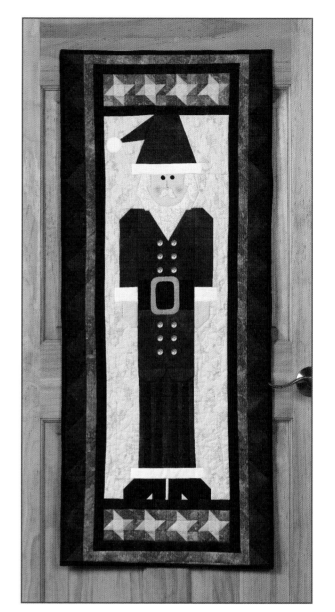

3. BORDER 1: Stitch strips end to end and trim to same length as quilt. Make 2. Stitch to sides of quilt. Press.

4. BORDER 2: Stitch strips end to end and trim to same length as quilt. Make 2. Stitch to sides of quilt. Repeat for top and bottom. Press.

5. BORDER 3: Make 24 units using directions for Border 3 on page 20. Stitch into 2 borders of 12 units each. Stitch to sides of quilt, oriented as shown. Press.

6. LAYER & QUILT: Trim backing to same size as batting. Layer and quilt as desired. Trim backing and batting even with quilt top.

7. BIND: Stitch binding strips end to end. Press in half lengthwise, wrong sides together. Bind quilt using ¼″ seam allowance.

2.

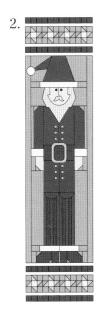

3-5.

Uncle Sam

Witch

Uncle Sam

Yardage Choose fabrics with 42″ usable width.

Background	½ yd
Shirt, hat, vest, cuffs, checkerboard	⅙ yd each of 3 fabrics
Pants	⅛ yd each of 2 fabrics
Shoes, eyes	⅛ yd
Face, hands	⅙ yd
Beard, mustache	¼ yd
Star appliques	⅛ yd

See Santa door hanging yardage on page 26 for star units, borders, binding, backing, and batting.

Use directions on page 5 for Uncle Sam block. Use directions for Santa door hanging on page 26 for other units and assembly.

Witch

Yardage Choose fabrics with 42″ usable width.

Background	½ yd
Dress, hat, lapels	⅜ yd
Vest/bodice, checkerboard	¼ yd
Shoes, eyes, checkerboard	⅙ yd
Socks	⅛ yd each of 2 fabrics
Face, hands, spider	⅙ yd
Stars, buttons, hair	⅛ yd each of 2 fabrics
Spider eyes - white	⅛ yd
Spider spots	⅛ yd

See Santa door hanging yardage on page 26 for star units, borders, binding, backing, and batting.

Use directions on page 9 for witch block. Use directions for Santa door hanging on page 26 for other units and assembly.

IMPORTANT: Directions are for fusible web applique, and patterns are reversed and ready to be traced. Be sure to have plenty of fusible web on hand.

47 x 55″   8″ Block

Yardage Choose fabrics with 42″ usable width.

Blocks   ⅛ yd each of 24 fabrics for centers & logs
⅙ yd each of 4 fabrics for last 2 logs in each block (darkest plum, orchid, blue-violet, & purple)
see block diagrams at right for colors

Applique   ⅛ yd each of 5 fabrics - hearts
⅙ yd each of 2 fabrics - leaves
⅜ yd - vine

Border 1   ⅓ yd
Border 2   ¼ yd
Border 3   1⅛ yd
Binding   ⅝ yd
Backing   3¼ yd
Batting   53 x 61″

Cutting Cut strips from selvage to selvage.

Blocks   centers - 1 square 2½″ for each block
logs - 1-3 strips 1½″ of each log fabric, as needed

Applique   18 hearts, 72 leaves - patterns on page 37
vine directions - see Step 5

Border 1   4 strips 2″ wide
Border 2   4-5 strips 1″ wide
Border 3   5-6 strips 6″ wide
Binding   6 strips 2½″ wide

Directions

Use ¼″ seam allowance unless otherwise noted.

1. BLOCKS: Refer to cutting chart and piecing diagrams on page 16 to make 20 blocks. Use diagrams at top right of this page and photo on page 29 for color placement. Press.

2. ASSEMBLE: Arrange blocks as shown. Stitch into rows. Press. Stitch rows together. Press.

3. BORDER 1: Stitch strips end to end and trim to same length as quilt. Make 2. Stitch to sides of quilt. Press. Repeat at top and bottom of quilt.

4. BORDERS 2 & 3: Repeat Step 3.

5. APPLIQUE: Bond 11 x 22″ of vine fabric with fusible web. Cut 18 **bias** pieces ⅜″ wide by 14″ long.

1.

Block 1
4 olives,
3 plums

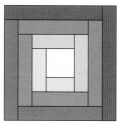

Make 5

Block 2
4 olives,
3 orchids

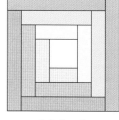

Make 5

Block 3
4 gray-teals,
3 blue-violets

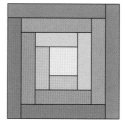

Make 5

Block 4
4 teals,
3 purples

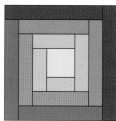

Make 5

2.

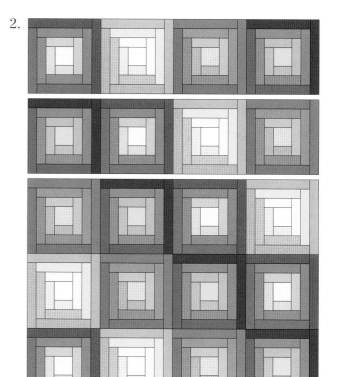

Continued on page 36

29

EASTER PARADE

40 x 43″

Yardage Choose fabrics with 42″ usable width.

Blocks	⅙ yd each of 24 or more fabrics
Sashing, Border 2	¼ yd each of 6 fabrics
Border 1, binding	¼ yd each of 4 fabrics
Backing	2⅞ yd
Batting	44 x 47″

Cutting Cut strips from selvage to selvage.

Blocks	see Step 1
Sashing	see Step 1
Border 1	1 strip 1½″ wide of each fabric
Border 2	1 strip 4½″ wide of each fabric
Binding	2 strips 2½″ wide of each fabric

Directions

Use ¼″ seam allowance unless otherwise noted.

1. BLOCKS & SASHING: Block names are followed by sizes of **finished** blocks for Easter Parade quilt including added sashing where required. Refer to page numbers following block sizes for cutting and assembly diagrams. Number of blocks to make follows page number. Next come sizes to cut extra sashing pieces. Diagrams for adding sashing pieces to blocks are at upper right.

   Log Cabin - 10″ - Page 16 - Make 1 - 2 pieces 1½ x 8½″, 2 pieces 1½ x 10½″

   House - 10″ - Page 21 - Make 1 - After pressing block, trim a bit off top and bottom to make block 10½″ from raw edge to raw edge.

   Four-patch Star - 10″ - Page 17 - Make 1 - 2 pieces 1½ x 8½″, 2 pieces 1½ x 10½″

   Bear Paw - 14″ - Page 20 (cut half the number of pieces listed in the chart) - Make 1 - 2 pieces 2¼ x 11″, 2 pieces 2¼ x 14½″

   Patchwork Hearts - 6 x 14″ - Page 18 - Make 2 - 2 pieces 1½ x 6½″

   Broken Dishes - 10 x 14″ - Page 19 - Make 1 - 4 pieces 1½ x 10½″

   Tiny Stars - 9″ - Page 4 - Make 1 block with 9 star units, alternating background fabrics.

   Nine-Patch Star - 9″ - Page 14 (cut one-third the number of pieces listed in the chart) - Make 1

   Pinwheels - 4 x 8″ - Page 15 - Make 2

Continued on page 36

1.

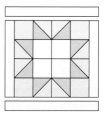

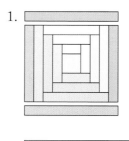

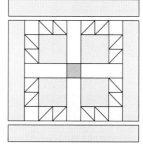

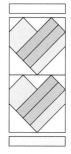

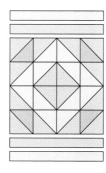

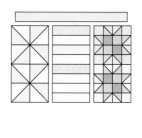

2.

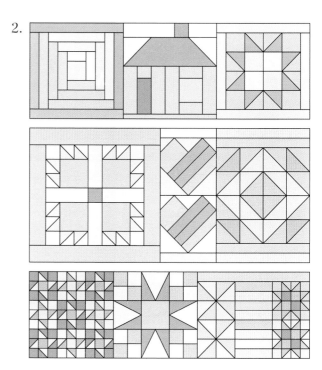

40 x 47″   6″ & 4″ Blocks

Yardage Choose fabrics with 42″ usable width.

Pink	¼ yd each of 5 or more fabrics
Orange	¼ yd each of 5 or more fabrics
White	1½ yd
Light orange	⅞ yd - sashing rectangles, Border 1, Border 3
Medium orange	⅛ yd - sashing squares
Binding	½ yd
Backing	2¾ yd
Batting	44 x 51″

Cutting Cut strips from selvage to selvage.

Heart block	see Step 1
Pinwheel block	see Step 1
Sashing	31 pieces 1¼ x 6½″
	12 squares 1¼″
Border 1	2 strips 1⅜″ wide - sides
	2 strips 1½″ wide - top & bottom
Border 2	30 pieces 1½ x 4½″ - pink
	32 pieces 1½ x 4½″ - orange
	64 pieces 1½ x 4½″ - white
Border 3	5 strips 2½″ wide
Binding	5 strips 2½″ wide

Directions

Use ¼″ seam allowance unless otherwise noted.

1. BLOCKS: Make 20 patchwork heart blocks, 10 facing left and 10 facing right. Make 4 pinwheel blocks. Use pink and orange fabrics as desired, using diagrams at right and photo on page 33 as guides. Refer to cutting charts and diagrams for patchwork hearts on page 18 and pinwheels on page 15. To use cutting charts effectively, cut and stitch 2 blocks at a time. Press.

2. ASSEMBLE: Stitch blocks into rows with sashing rectangles, alternating left and right facing blocks. Press. Stitch rows of sashing rectangles and sashing squares together. Press. Stitch rows of blocks and rows of sashing together. Press.

3. BORDER 1: Cut border strips to fit sides of quilt. Stitch to quilt. Press. Repeat at top and bottom of quilt. Press.

4. BORDER 2: Make 2 side borders with 35 pieces, alternating colors as shown. Press. Make 2 top/ bottom borders with 28 pieces, alternating colors as

1.

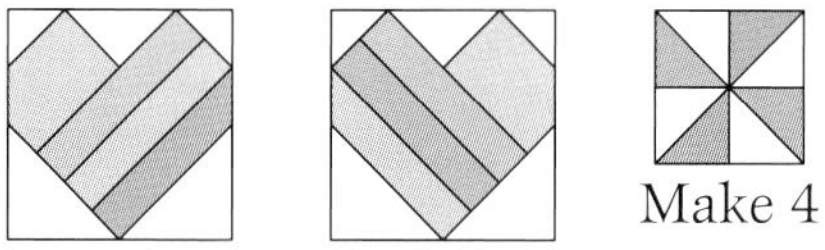

Make 10   Make 10   Make 4

2.

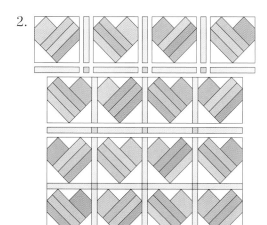

4. Sides - 35 pieces - Make 2

Top & bottom - 28 pieces - Make 2

4.

   Continued on page 36

WATERMELON STARS

52 x 60″   8″ Block

Yardage *Choose fabrics with 42″ usable width.*

Pink	⅙ yd each of 15 or more fabrics - light, medium
	⅙ yd each of 2 or more fabrics - dark
Green	⅙ yd each of 15 or more fabrics - light, medium
	⅙ yd each of 2 or more fabrics - dark
Border 1	½ yd
Border 3	1⅓ yd
Binding	⅝ yd
Backing	3½ yd
Batting	58 x 66″

Cutting *Cut strips from selvage to selvage.*

Units A & B	*1⅞″ squares - 120 pink, 40 green (med, dk)
	1½″ squares - 80 pink, 80 green (med, dk)
Blocks, Bdr 2	*2⅞″ squares - 120 pink, 120 green (lt, med)
	2½″ squares - 44 pink, 40 green (lt, med)
Border 1	4 strips 2½″ wide
Border 3	6 strips 6½″ wide
Binding	6-7 strips 2½″ wide

*Cut in **half** diagonally.

Directions

Use ¼″ seam allowance unless otherwise noted.

1. CENTER UNITS: Using diagrams at right and photo on page 35 for color and value placement, make 20 units. Refer to cutting chart above and diagrams for 4″ four-patch stars on page 15.

   Unit A: Make 10 units with green side triangles and pink corner squares.

   Unit B: Make 10 units with pink side triangles and green corner squares.

2. BLOCKS: Using diagrams at right and photo on page 35 for color and value placement, make 20 blocks. Refer to diagrams for 8″ four-patch stars on page 17. Use 4″ star units from Step 1 for centers.

   Block A: Make 10 blocks with green star points, pink side triangles, pink corner squares, and Unit A centers.

   Block B: Make 10 blocks with pink star points, green side triangles, green corner squares, and Unit B centers.

3. ASSEMBLE: Stitch blocks into rows as shown, alternating Blocks A and B. Press. Stitch rows together. Press.

1.

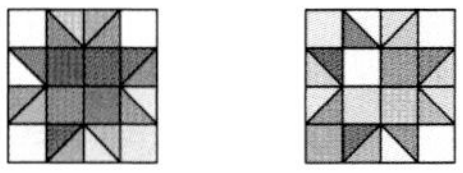

   Unit A   Unit B
   Make 10   Make 10

2.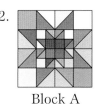

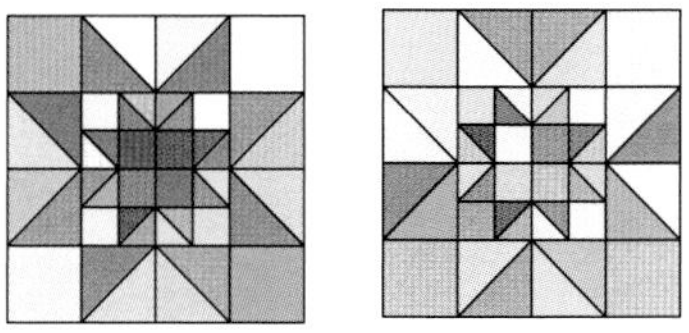

   Block A   Block B
   Make 10   Make 10

3.

5.

Sides - Make 2 borders with 22 units each, changing direction at center

Top/bottom - Make 2 borders with 18 units each, changing direction at center - add 2½″ pink squares to each end

4. BORDER 1: Stitch strips end to end and trim to same length as quilt. Make 2. Stitch to sides of quilt. Press. Repeat at top and bottom of quilt. Press.

5. BORDER 2: Make 80 half-square triangle units with triangles cut from 2⅞″ squares. Press. Make borders as shown above. Stitch side borders to quilt first, then top and bottom. Press.

6. BORDER 3: Repeat Step 4.

7. LAYER & QUILT: Piece backing horizontally to same size as batting. Layer and quilt as desired. Trim backing and batting even with quilt top.

8. BIND: Stitch binding strips end to end. Press in half lengthwise, wrong sides together. Bind quilt using ⅜″ seam allowance.

Summer Hydrangea

Continued from page 28

Arrange vine sections, curving casually. Trim ends as needed. Cover ends of each vine section with hearts. Add leaves. Fuse.

6. LAYER & QUILT: Piece backing horizontally to same size as batting. Layer and quilt as desired. Trim backing and batting even with quilt top.

7. BIND: Stitch binding strips end to end. Press in half lengthwise, wrong sides together. Bind quilt using ⅜″ seam allowance.

Sherbet Hearts

Continued from page 32

shown. Press. Stitch side borders to quilt as shown in diagram on page 32. Press. Stitch pinwheels to each end of top and bottom borders, borders and blocks oriented as shown in diagram. Press. Stitch top and bottom borders to quilt. Press.

5. BORDER 3: Repeat Step 3.

6. LAYER & QUILT: Piece backing horizontally to same size as batting. Layer and quilt as desired. Trim backing and batting even with quilt top.

7. BIND: Stitch binding strips end to end. Press in half lengthwise, wrong sides together. Bind quilt using ⅜″ seam allowance.

Easter Parade

Continued from page 30

Bars Unit - 4 x 8″ - Page 16 - Make 1 - Use 8 pieces rather than 10.

Four-patch Star 4″ - 4 x 8″ - Page 15 (cut half the number of pieces listed in the chart) - Make 2 Cut sashing strip 1½ x 12½″. Assemble with pinwheels and bars unit as shown at top right on page 30 (unit finished size 12 x 9″).

2. ASSEMBLE: Stitch blocks into rows as shown. Press. Stitch rows together. Press.

3. BORDER 1: Stitch side borders to quilt. Press. Stitch top and bottom borders to quilt. Press.

4. BORDER 2: Repeat Step 3.

5. LAYER & QUILT: Piece backing vertically to same size as batting. Layer and quilt as desired. Trim backing and batting even with quilt top.

6. BIND: Cut binding strips into 7-12″ segments. Stitch binding strips end to end, alternating colors, and using seams with a 45° angle. Trim seam allowances to ¼″ and press open. Press strip in half lengthwise, wrong sides together. Bind quilt using ⅜″ seam allowance.

Ideas for More Seasonal Delights
Make larger wall hangings by adding a border or two

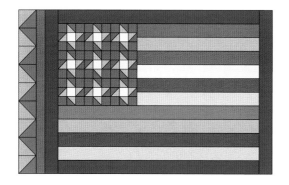

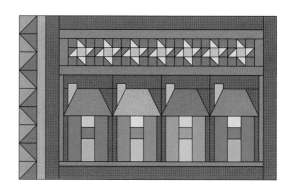

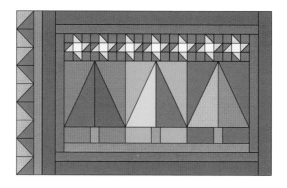

Heart Flower
Block

1776

Let Freedom
Ring Block

1776

Peace on
Earth Block

Joy

Applique patterns are
for fusible web–reversed
for tracing & no seam
allowances added

Summer
Hydrangea

Santa Block *Joy*

Jacket Flap

37

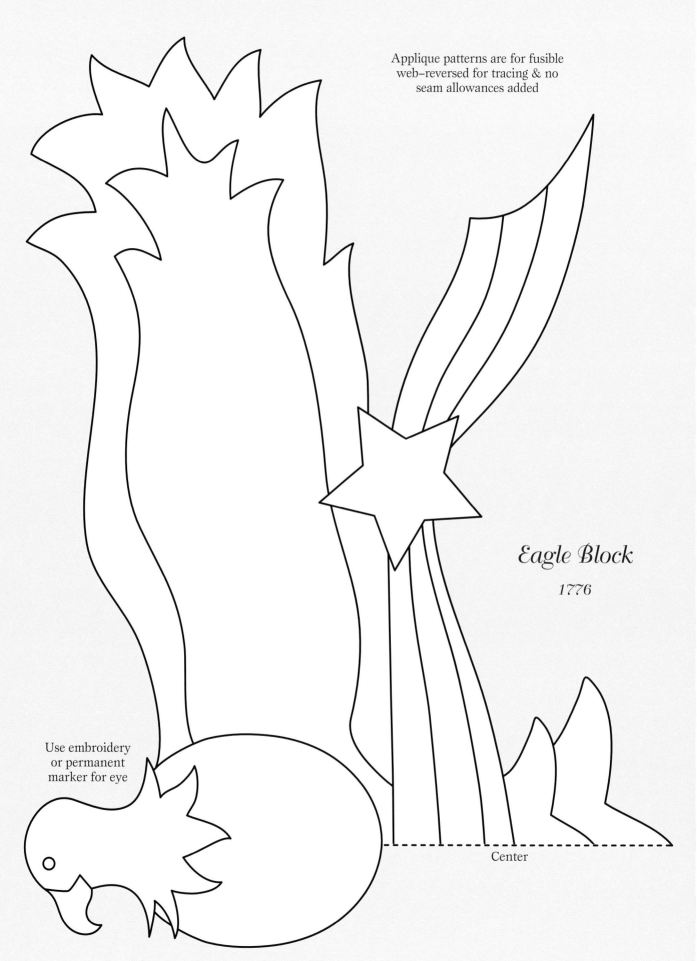

Applique patterns are for fusible
web–reversed for tracing & no
seam allowances added

Eagle Block

1776

Use embroidery
or permanent
marker for eye

Center

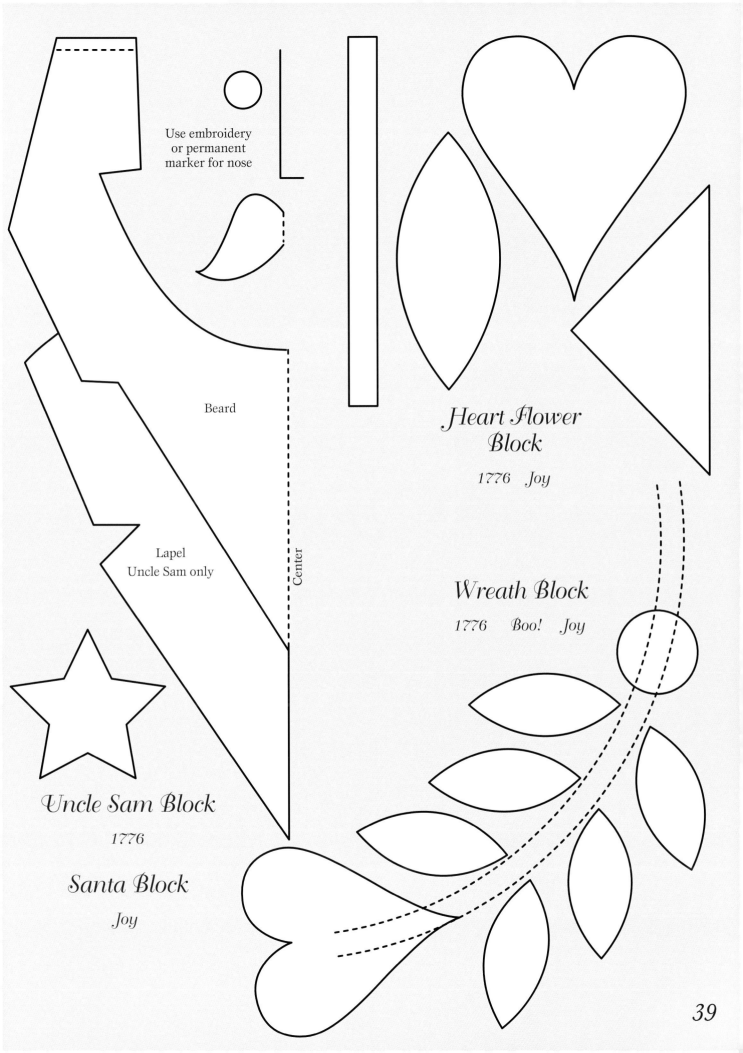

Use embroidery
or permanent
marker for nose

Beard

Center

Lapel
Uncle Sam only

*Heart Flower
Block*

1776   Joy

Wreath Block

1776   Boo!   Joy

Uncle Sam Block

1776

Santa Block

Joy

39

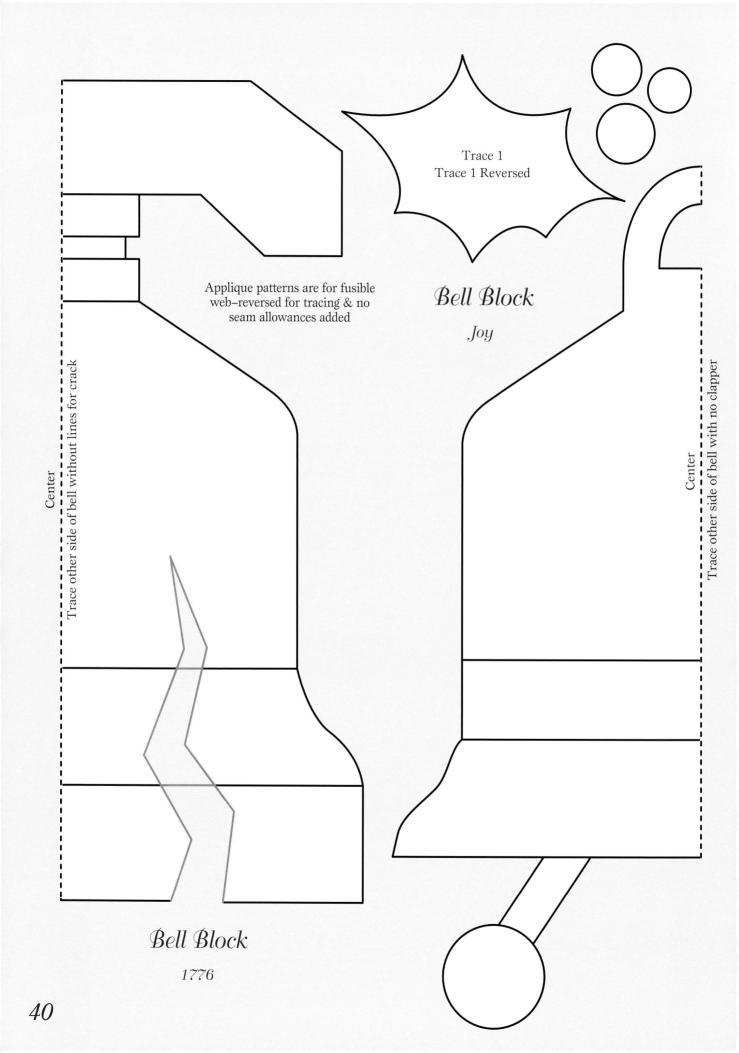

Trace 1
Trace 1 Reversed

Applique patterns are for fusible
web–reversed for tracing & no
seam allowances added

Bell Block

Joy

Center

Trace other side of bell without lines for crack

Center

Trace other side of bell with no clapper

Bell Block

1776

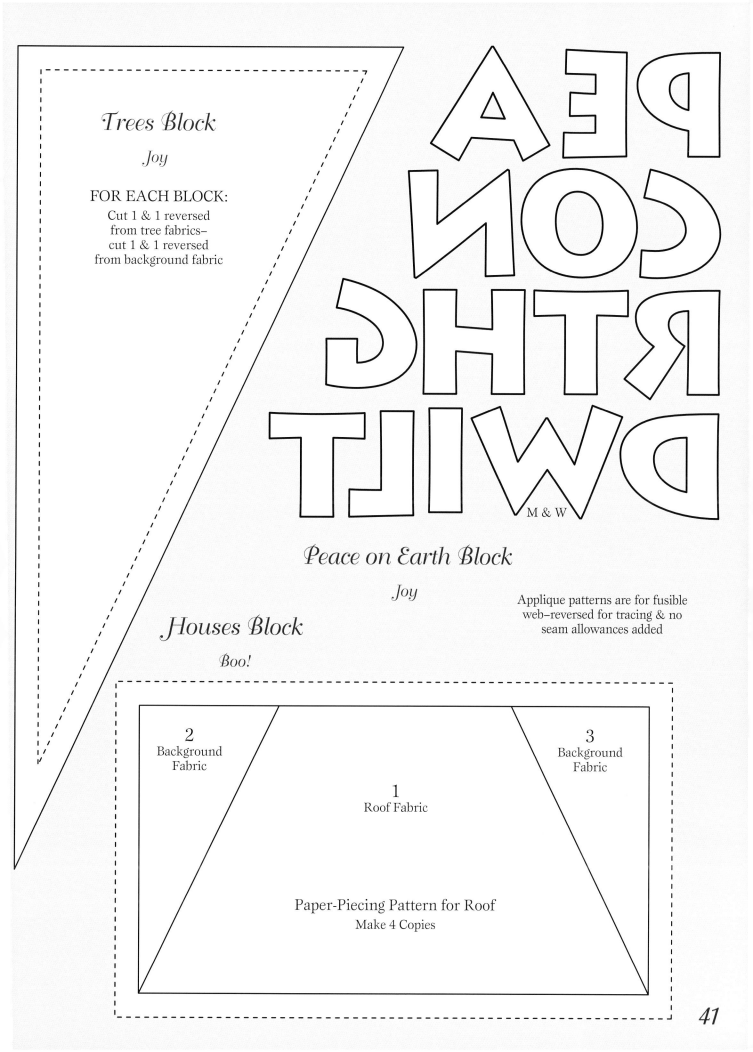

Trees Block

Joy

FOR EACH BLOCK:
Cut 1 & 1 reversed
from tree fabrics–
cut 1 & 1 reversed
from background fabric

PEACON RTHG DWILT

M & W

Peace on Earth Block

Joy

Applique patterns are for fusible
web–reversed for tracing & no
seam allowances added

Houses Block

Boo!

2
Background
Fabric

3
Background
Fabric

1
Roof Fabric

Paper-Piecing Pattern for Roof
Make 4 Copies

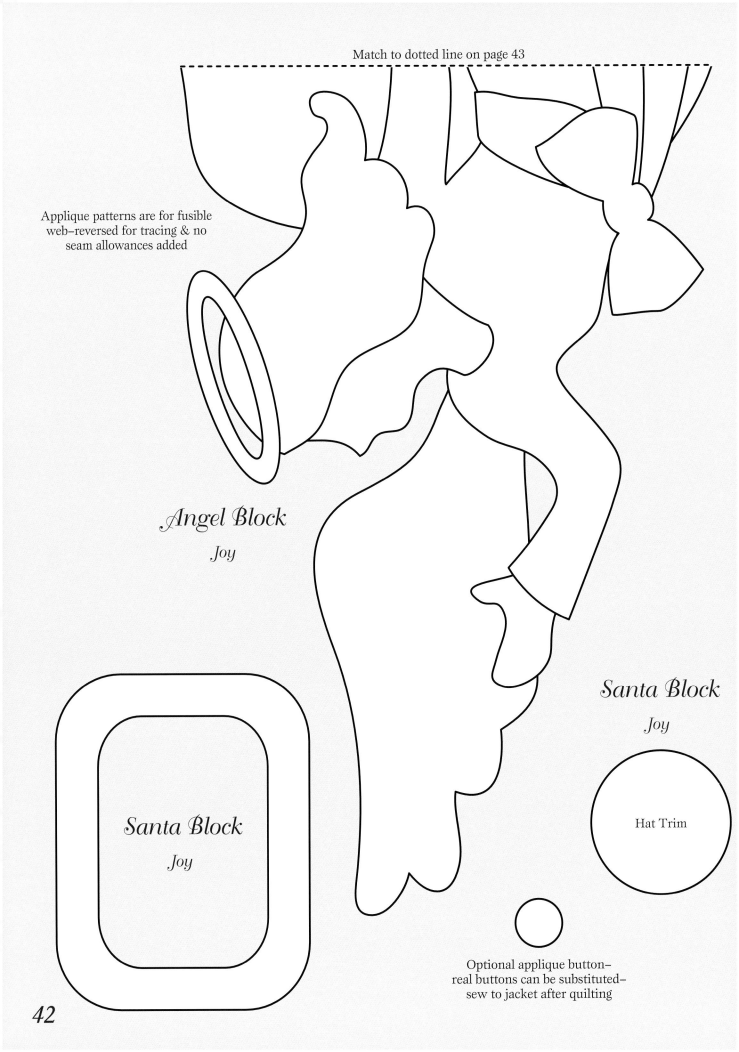

Match to dotted line on page 43

Applique patterns are for fusible
web–reversed for tracing & no
seam allowances added

Angel Block

Joy

Santa Block

Joy

Santa Block

Joy

Hat Trim

Optional applique button–
real buttons can be substituted–
sew to jacket after quilting

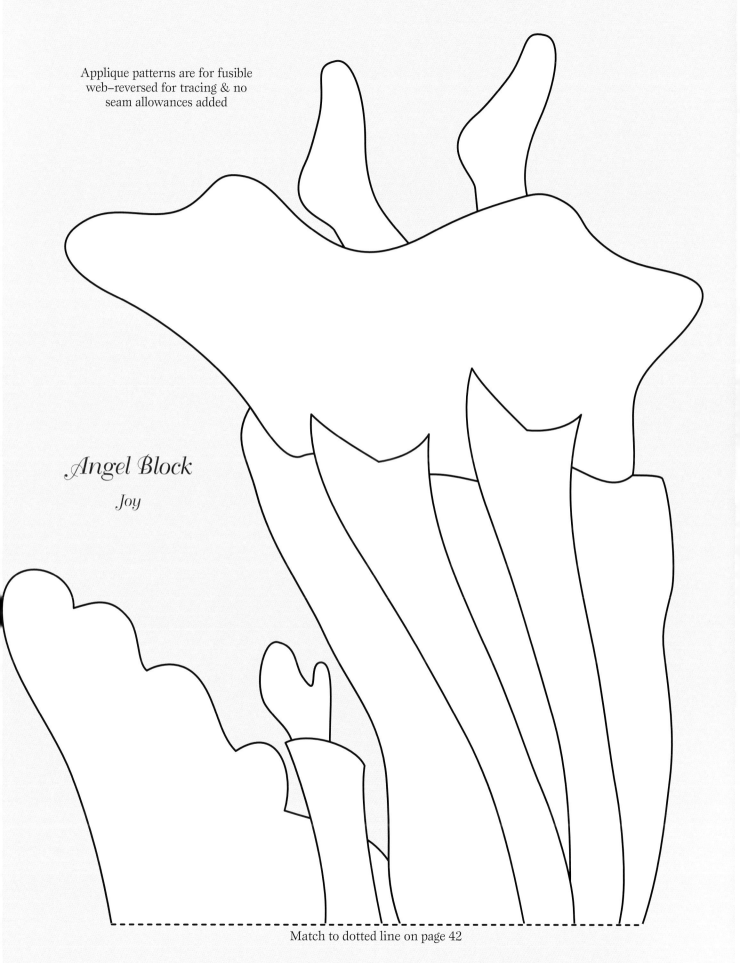

Applique patterns are for fusible
web–reversed for tracing & no
seam allowances added

Angel Block

Joy

Match to dotted line on page 42

43

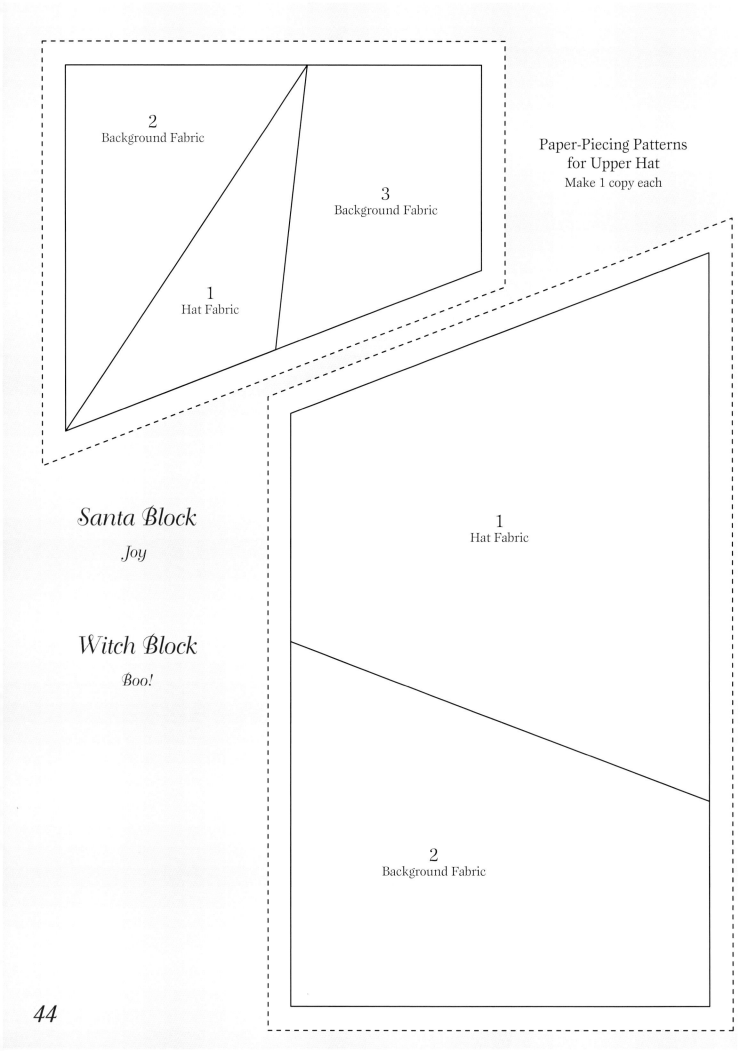

2
Background Fabric

3
Background Fabric

1
Hat Fabric

Paper-Piecing Patterns
for Upper Hat
Make 1 copy each

Santa Block

Joy

Witch Block

Boo!

1
Hat Fabric

2
Background Fabric

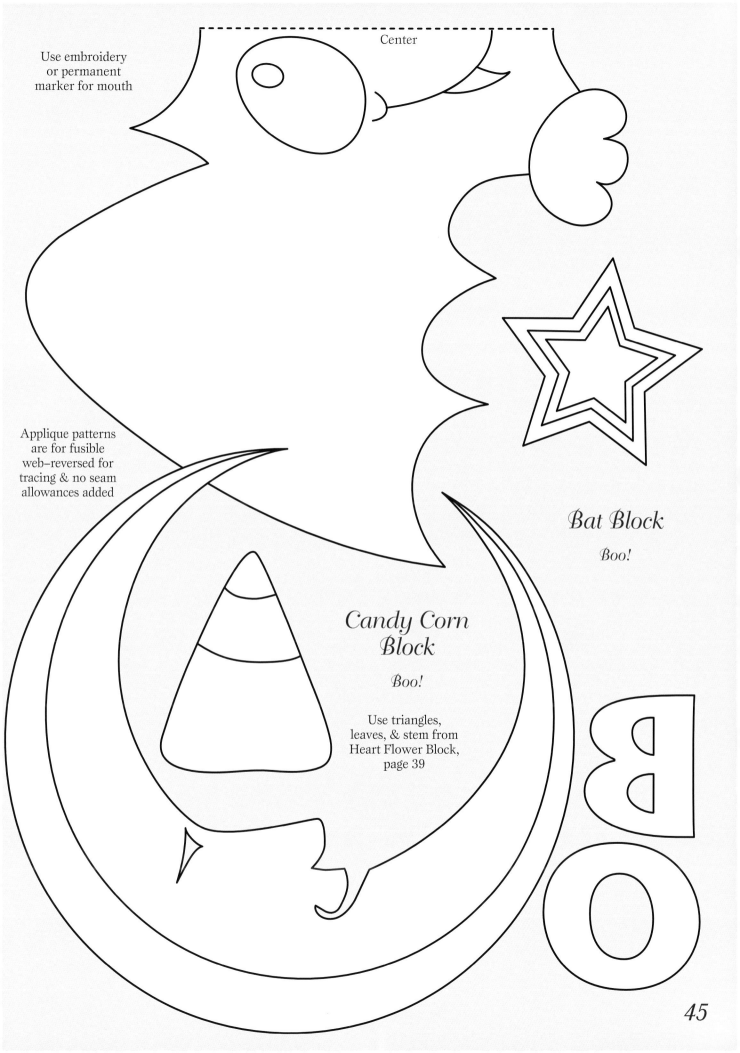

Center

Use embroidery
or permanent
marker for mouth

Applique patterns
are for fusible
web–reversed for
tracing & no seam
allowances added

Bat Block

Boo!

Candy Corn
Block

Boo!

Use triangles,
leaves, & stem from
Heart Flower Block,
page 39

45

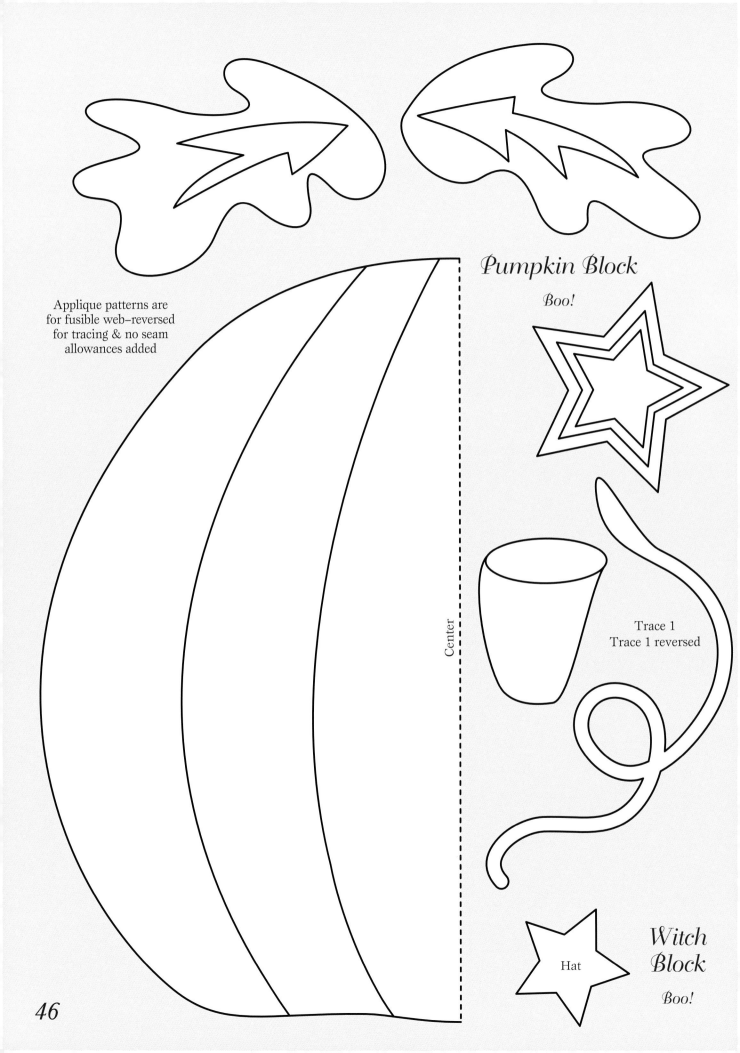

Applique patterns are
for fusible web–reversed
for tracing & no seam
allowances added

Pumpkin Block

Boo!

Center

Trace 1
Trace 1 reversed

Hat

*Witch
Block*

Boo!

46

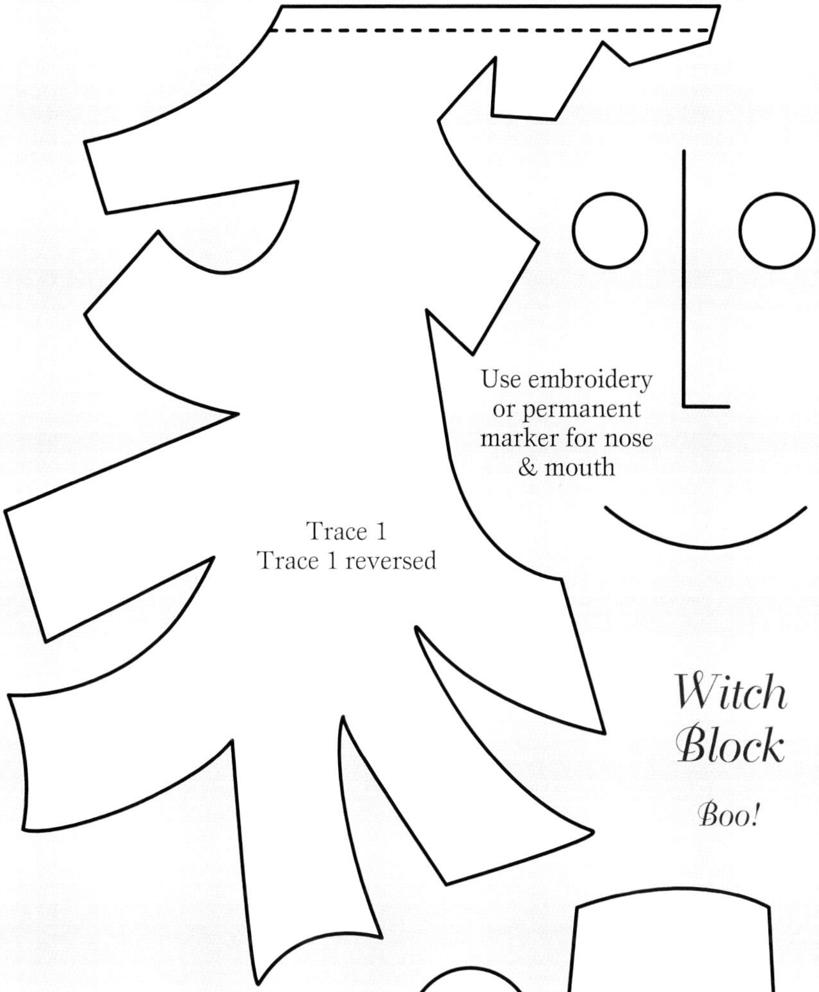

HAPPY HAUNTING UNDITCH

Use embroidery or permanent marker for nose & mouth

Trace 1
Trace 1 reversed

Witch Block

Boo!

Happy Haunting Block

Boo!

Optional applique button–
real buttons can be substituted–
sew to vest after quilting

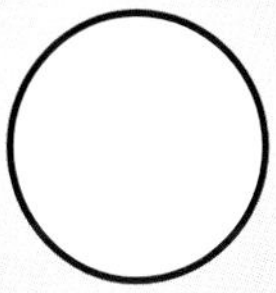

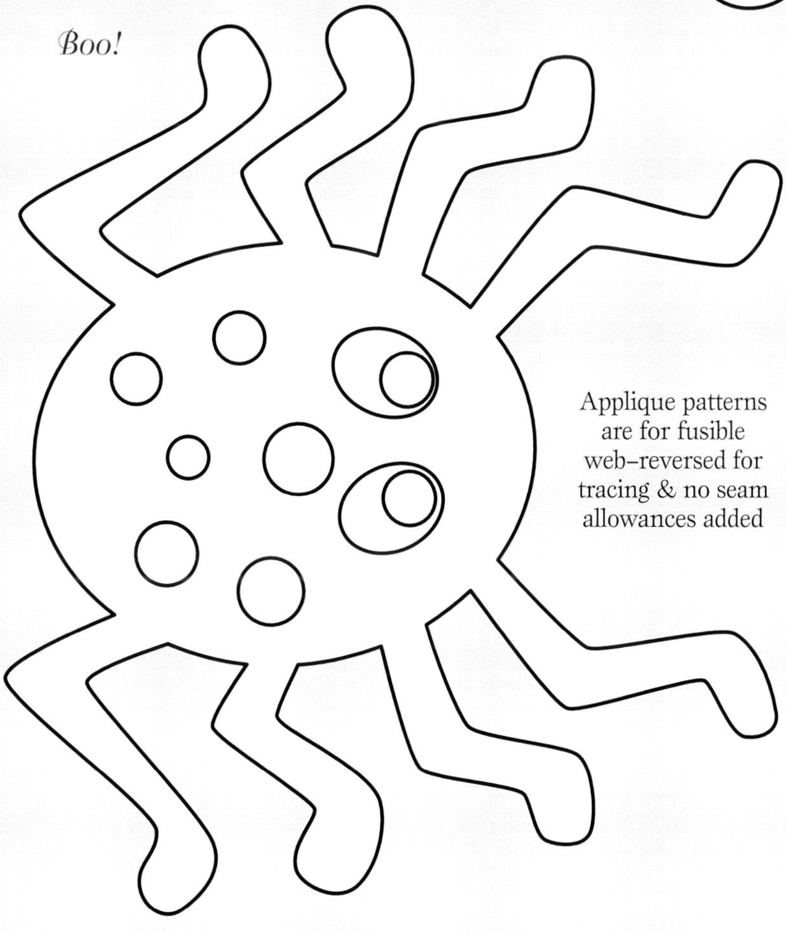

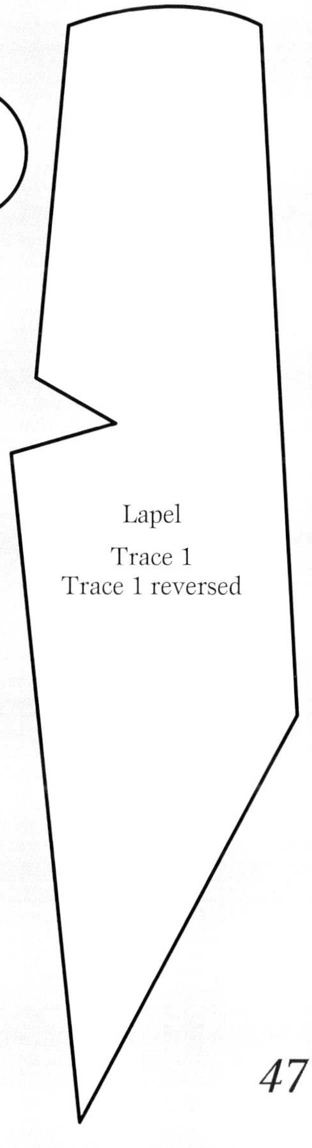

Lapel
Trace 1
Trace 1 reversed

Applique patterns
are for fusible
web–reversed for
tracing & no seam
allowances added

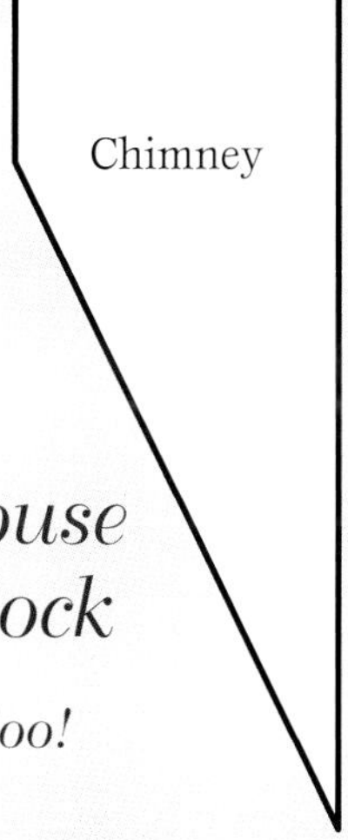

Chimney

House Block

Boo!

47